Our Journey to You

a newborn adoption memory book

for

_____

created by Susan Rutledge

WILLOW
BEND
PRESS

Our Journey To You, A Newborn Adoption Memory Book
Copyright © 2019 by Susan Rutledge. All rights reserved.
No part of this publication may be reproduced, stored in a retrieval system or transmitted, in any form or by any means - electronic, mechanical, photocopying, recording or otherwise, without prior written permission from the publisher, except for the inclusion of brief quotations in a review.

All Scripture quotations, unless otherwise indicated, are taken from The Holy Bible, New International Version®, NIV® Copyright © 1973, 1978, 1984, 2011 by Biblica, Inc.® Used by permission. All rights reserved worldwide.

Scripture quotations marked ESV are from the ESV® Bible (The Holy Bible, English Standard Version®), copyright © 2001 by Crossway, a publishing ministry of Good News Publishers. Used by permission. All rights reserved.

Cover photograph by Nathan Dumlao

Published by Willow Bend Press
willowbendpress.com

Paperback ISBN-13: 978-1-950019-04-5
Hardback ISBN-13: 978-1-950019-05-2

First Printing February 2019

Cover, Interior Design and Illustrations by Susan Rutledge

www.susanrutledge.com

Dedication

To Becky & Aaron...may all
of your prayers be answered
and your dreams
come true

Table of Contents

About the Author _____ 6
A Note About the Format _____ 7
   Our Journey Begins _____ 9
   We Want To Adopt! _____ 10
   The Perfect Match _____ 12
   Your Birth Family _____ 13
   Before You Were Born _____ 14
   Our Prayers For You _____ 16
   Scriptures for Our Family _____ 17
   Special Photos _____ 18
   Before There Was You _____ 19
   Trivia & Facts About Mom _____ 20
   Mom's Family Tree _____ 21
   Trivia & Facts About Dad _____ 22
   Dad's Family Tree _____ 23
   Mom & Dad's Love Story _____ 24
   Mom's Love Letter to You _____ 26
   Dad's Love Letter to You _____ 27
   Your Birth _____ 28
   Your Hand & Feet Prints _____ 30
   Your Hospital Stay _____ 31
   Names We Liked _____ 32
   Visitors & Gifts _____ 33
   It Was Love At First Sight _____ 34
   You Are Adorable! _____ 35
   On the Day You Were Born _____ 36
   Coming Home _____ 37
   A Typical Day At Our House _____ 38

Table of Contents

Your First Outings 39

Milestones 40

Your Favorites 41

Moments We Want to Remember 42

Cousins, Aunts & Uncles 43

Adoption Finalization 44

Gotcha Day 45

Your First Trips by Land 46

Your First Trips by Sea & Air 47

Your First Christmas 48

You Bring Joy to Our World! 49

Your Teething Chart 50

Medical Records 51

State Where You Live 52

States You Have Visited 53

Your First Year 54

You Are Growing 55

Friends, Neighbors & Play Dates 56

Your Reaction to the Seasons 57

Family Vacations 58

Family Pics 59

Birthday Parties 60

Party Pics 61

From Our Hearts to Yours 63
    Journal entries documenting emotions and experiences before, during and after the adoption process, along with hopes and dreams for the growing family's future.

About the Author

Susan Rutledge, a graduate of Oklahoma State University, spent over thirty years working with children and families in church ministry before retiring in 2011 to pursue her passion for writing. Her published titles include Barely a Bunny, Marvin Maples Told a Lie, Have You Seen the Missing Letter A?, Ty the Turtle in the Land of the Can'ts, The Cares & Prayers Journal for Tweens and Simple Words to Love By.

Mrs. Rutledge enjoys speaking to all ages about her books and is available for book readings, assemblies, seminars, classroom instruction and book signings.

In addition to publishing books, Susan regularly blogs about her life experiences as a mother and grandmother. She and her husband, Grant live in Prosper, Texas. They have four married children and ten grandchildren.

For more information, visit susanrutledge.com

A Note About the Format

Be sure to work on both sections at the same time!!!

Section 1 - The Journey Begins (Pages 9-61)

This section records information about the adoption process, the birth, coming home, all the "firsts" and other details and fun information about your child and family. Read through the pages often for reminders of what to watch for so everything is documented. Several pages are dedicated to photographs. Take the time to print out some of your digital snapshots and don't leave these pages blank. You'll be glad later when you sit down to look through this book with your son or daughter!

Section 2 - From Our Heart to Yours (Pages 63-99)

These pages are for you to journal your feelings, your hopes, your dreams, your frustrations, your fears...your hearts. Entries don't have to be long, but they will be special for your child to read some day. Consider writing about the highs and lows you've experienced during the adoption process, the challenges, the excitement, the prayers and the answers...all these emotions are a part of your child's story. Preserve as many as you can, to give your child an understanding of the depth of your love and dedication to them.

Space is provided for nearly 150 entries. Date each one and if both parents are journaling, be sure to sign them! Begin journaling now...and never stop. When you run out of room in this memory book, buy a notebook and keep going!

Our Journey Begins

The Story of You

Our journey to you began long before you were even born. This is your story...from the beginning. We marvel how God orchestrated circumstances to join our lives together and will be forever grateful to Him and everyone else involved. One day we will sit and read this book and reminisce with you about your birth and early childhood. It will be fun to share the stories and our memories of you...our little miracle. For now, we will work at filling in the blanks, along with changing your diapers, rocking you in the night, comforting you when you cry, singing you silly nursery songs, washing your clothes, walking you in the park, praying for you, standing nearby to catch you when you fall, feeding you when you are hungry, teaching you your ABC's, and the other gazillion things mommies and daddies get to do. We know time will quickly pass and you won't be little forever. With joy and pride, we will watch you grow and cherish every moment God gives us with you!

We Want To Adopt!

Why we chose to adopt _____
_____
_____
_____
_____
_____

Steps we took to begin the journey _____
_____
_____
_____
_____
_____
_____
_____
_____

Highlights from our parenting classes _____
_____
_____
_____
_____
_____
_____

Class Notes
- Love unconditionally
- Listen to your child
- Tuck them in bed every night
- Discipline in love
- Support their talents
- Encourage their dreams
- Be a good role model

What we did to prepare for our Home Study _____

The Home Study _____

Special people who helped us _____

The Perfect Match

How we first found out about you

_____
_____
_____
_____
_____
_____
_____
_____
_____
_____
_____
_____
_____
_____

Conversations with your birth mother

_____
_____
_____
_____
_____
_____
_____
_____
_____
_____
_____
_____
_____
_____

How it felt knowing we were chosen to be your forever mommy and daddy

_____
_____
_____
_____
_____
_____

Your Birth Family

Before You Were Born

Your due date _____

Doctor visits _____
_____
_____
_____
_____
_____
_____
_____
_____
_____
_____

Boy or girl? How and when we found out _____
_____
_____
_____
_____

How we felt when we saw the first sonogram picture of you _____
_____
_____
_____
_____
_____

How we told other people _____
_____
_____
_____
_____
_____
_____
_____
_____
_____

The first toy we bought for you was _____
_____
_____

The first piece of clothing we bought for you was _____
_____
_____

How we prepared for your homecoming _____
_____
_____
_____
_____
_____
_____
_____
_____

Checklist
- ☑ Diapers
- ☑ Baby Bed
- ☑ Car Seat
- ☑ Stroller
- ☑ Bottles
- ☑ Onesies
- ☑ Blankets
- ☑ Sheets
- ☑ Burp Rags
- ☑ Rocking Chair

Our Prayers For You

Your childhood _____
_____
_____
_____

Your friends _____
_____
_____
_____

Your teachers _____
_____
_____
_____

Your faith _____
_____
_____
_____

Your character _____
_____
_____
_____

Your purpose in life _____
_____
_____
_____

Scriptures for Our Family

"But as for me and my household, we will serve the Lord."
~Joshua 24:15

"Love the Lord your God with all your heart and with all your soul and with all your strength. These commandments that I give you today are to be on your hearts. Impress them on your children. Talk about them when you sit at home and when you walk along the road, when you lie down and when you get up. Tie them as symbols on your hands and bind them on your foreheads. Write them on the doorframes of your house and on your gates."
~Deuteronomy 6:6-9 NIV

"...Everyone should be quick to listen, slow to speak and slow to become angry."
~James 1:19b NIV

"Be completely humble and gentle; be patient, bearing with one another in love. Make every effort to keep the unity of the Spirit through the bond of peace."
~Ephesians 4:2-3

"Be kind and compassionate to one another, forgiving each other, just as in Christ God forgave you."
~Ephesians 4:32

Special Photos
Sonograms, Special Gifts, Etc.

Before There Was You

Pictures of Us

Trivia & Facts About Mom

Birthdate _____
Birthplace _____
Places Mom lived _____
_____

Schools Mom attended _____
_____

Mom's favorite hobbies _____
_____
_____

Mom's favorite foods _____
_____
_____

Mom's hero (and why) _____
_____
_____

Mom's first car _____
Mom's favorite book _____
Mom's favorite movie _____
Mom's favorite food _____
Mom's favorite Bible verse _____
_____
_____
_____
_____

Mom's Family Tree

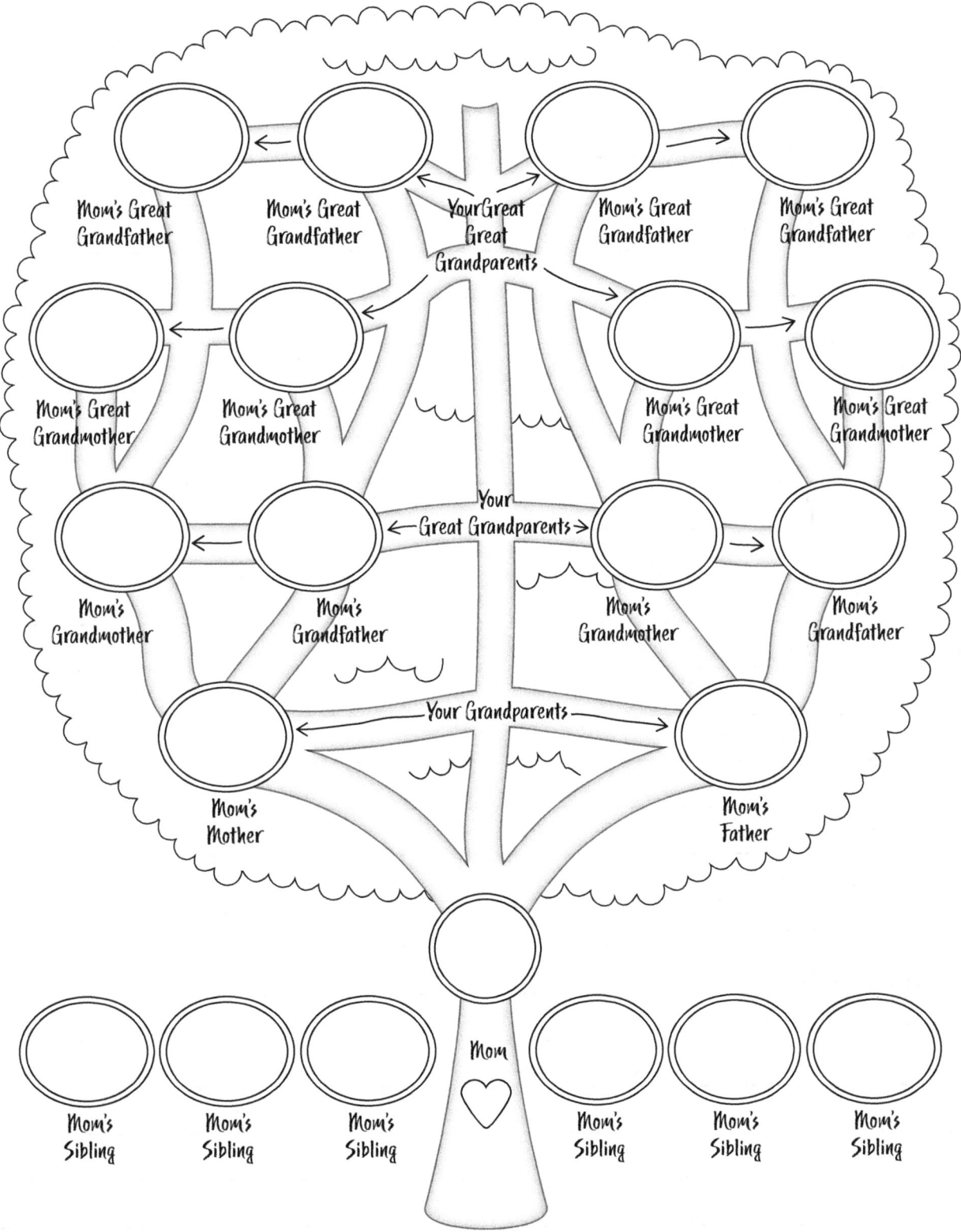

Trivia & Facts About Dad

Birthdate _____

Birthplace _____

Places Dad lived _____
_____
_____

Schools Dad attended _____
_____

Dad's favorite hobbies _____
_____
_____

Dad's favorite foods _____
_____
_____

Dad's hero (and why) _____
_____
_____
_____

Dad's first car _____
Dad's favorite book _____
Dad's favorite movie _____
Dad's favorite food _____
Dad's favorite Bible verse _____
_____
_____
_____
_____

Dad's Family Tree

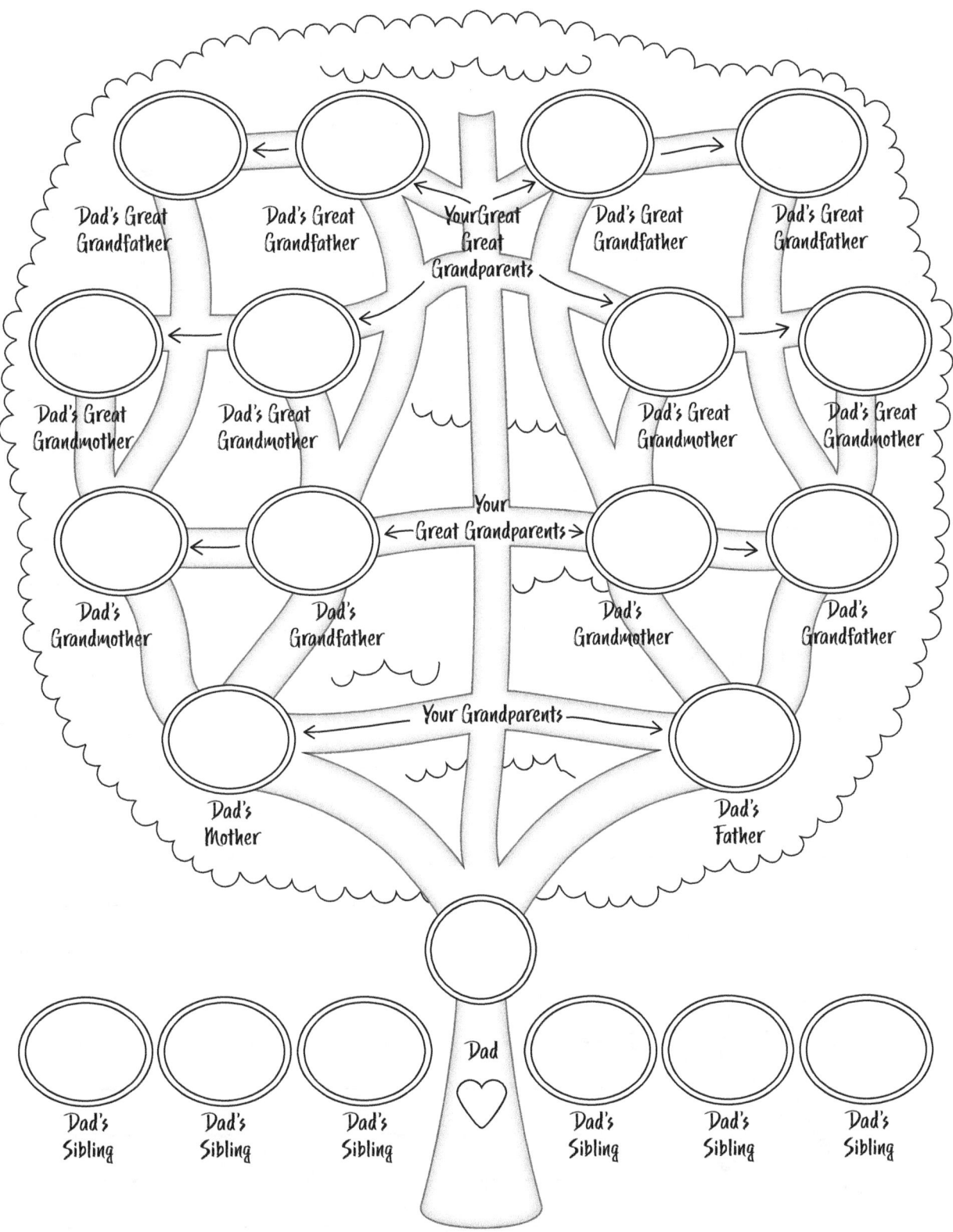

Mom & Dad's Love Story

Where we met _____

_____

How we met _____

_____

_____

_____

Our first date _____

_____

_____

_____

_____

Our favorite restaurants _____

_____

_____

Our favorite things to do together _____

_____

_____

_____

_____

_____

When we knew we were in love _____

_____

_____

_____

_____

_____

_____

_____

The proposal _____
_____
_____
_____
_____
_____

Our wedding _____
_____
_____
_____
_____
_____
_____

Our honeymoon _____
_____
_____
_____
_____
_____
_____

Favorite vacations _____
_____
_____
_____
_____
_____
_____
_____

Mom's Love Letter to You

Dad's Love Letter to You

Your Birth

Important Statistics

Date _____ Time _____
Weight _____ Length _____
Head measurement _____ Chest measurement _____
Hair color _____ Eye color _____

Hospital and city where you were born _____
_____

The weather that day _____
_____

The doctor who delivered you _____
_____

Family and friends who were there when you were born _____
_____
_____
_____
_____

What we did while we were waiting _____
_____
_____
_____
_____
_____

The first time we held you _____

_____
_____
_____
_____
_____
_____

The first person to pray for you _____

_____
_____
_____

Hospital guests _____

_____
_____
_____
_____
_____
_____

Now that you're here, we want you to know... _____

_____
_____
_____
_____
_____
_____
_____
_____
_____

Your Hand & Feet Prints

left hand   right hand

left foot   right foot

date _____

Your Hospital Stay

Names We Liked

Boy names | Girl names

Prince | *Princess*

First and middle names we chose _____
Meaning of the names _____
_____
_____
Why we chose your name _____
_____
_____

FIRST CHOICE

Visitors & Gifts

It Was Love At First Sight

First Pictures

You Are Adorable!
From Your Head to your Toes

On the Day You Were Born

Day of the week _____
President of the United States _____
Your birthstone _____
In the headlines _____
_____

The newest technology gadgets _____
_____
_____

Popular toys _____
_____
_____

Popular television shows _____
_____
_____

Famous people who share your birthday _____
_____
_____

New York Times #1 Best Selling Book _____
Billboards #1 Song _____
Top Box Office Movie _____
Cost of First Class postage stamp _____
Cost of a gallon of gasoline_____
Cost of a loaf of bread _____
Cost of a candy bar _____
Cost of a Happy Meal _____
Cost of a ticket to Disney World _____

Coming Home

Date _____

Address _____

City and state _____

What you wore _____

_____

Our transportation was _____

_____

What we did _____

_____

_____

Where you slept the first night _____

How it felt to bring you home _____

_____

_____

_____

_____

_____

A Typical Day At Our House

Your First Outings

To Grandparent's house _____
_____
_____
_____

To Church _____
_____
_____
_____

To the park _____
_____
_____
_____

Shopping _____
_____
_____

To the doctor _____
_____
_____
_____

The funniest thing happened when _____
_____
_____
_____
_____

Milestones

| First smiled | First held up head | First laughed | First rolled over |

| First reached for toy | First slept all night | First sat up | First crawled |

| First stood alone | First took a step | First fed yourself | First waved |

| First haircut | First taste of ice cream | First said a prayer | First used potty |

Your first words _____
First Halloween costume _____
First babysitter(s) _____
First pet(s) _____
Other firsts _____
_____
_____
_____

Your Favorites

Blankie _____

Toy(s) _____

Places to sleep _____

Foods _____

Songs _____

People _____

Times to play _____

Pacifier/thumb/other? _____

Bedtime Story _____

Sounds to make _____

Things to do _____

Things that make you laugh _____

_____

_____

_____

Moments We Want to Remember

First games you played _____
_____
_____
_____
_____

First time you said Dada _____
_____
_____
_____
_____

First time you said Mama _____
_____
_____
_____
_____

First night away from mom and dad _____
_____
_____
_____
_____

First time in the pool _____
_____
_____
_____
_____

Cousins, Aunts & Uncles

Adoption Finalization

Date _____

Location _____

_____

Judge _____

Who was with us _____

_____

Details _____

there was a missing piece in our family and we realized it was you!

you!

Gotcha Day
Photos of the Day You Officially Became Ours

Your First Trips by Land

Your First Trips by Sea & Air

Your First Christmas

Where we celebrated _____
_____
_____

What you wore _____
_____
_____

Toys & gifts we bought you _____
_____
_____
_____

Gifts you received from others _____
_____
_____
_____
_____

Our best "First Christmas" memories _____
_____
_____
_____
_____
_____
_____
_____

Christmas

You Bring Joy to Our World!
Christmas Pictures

Your Teething Chart

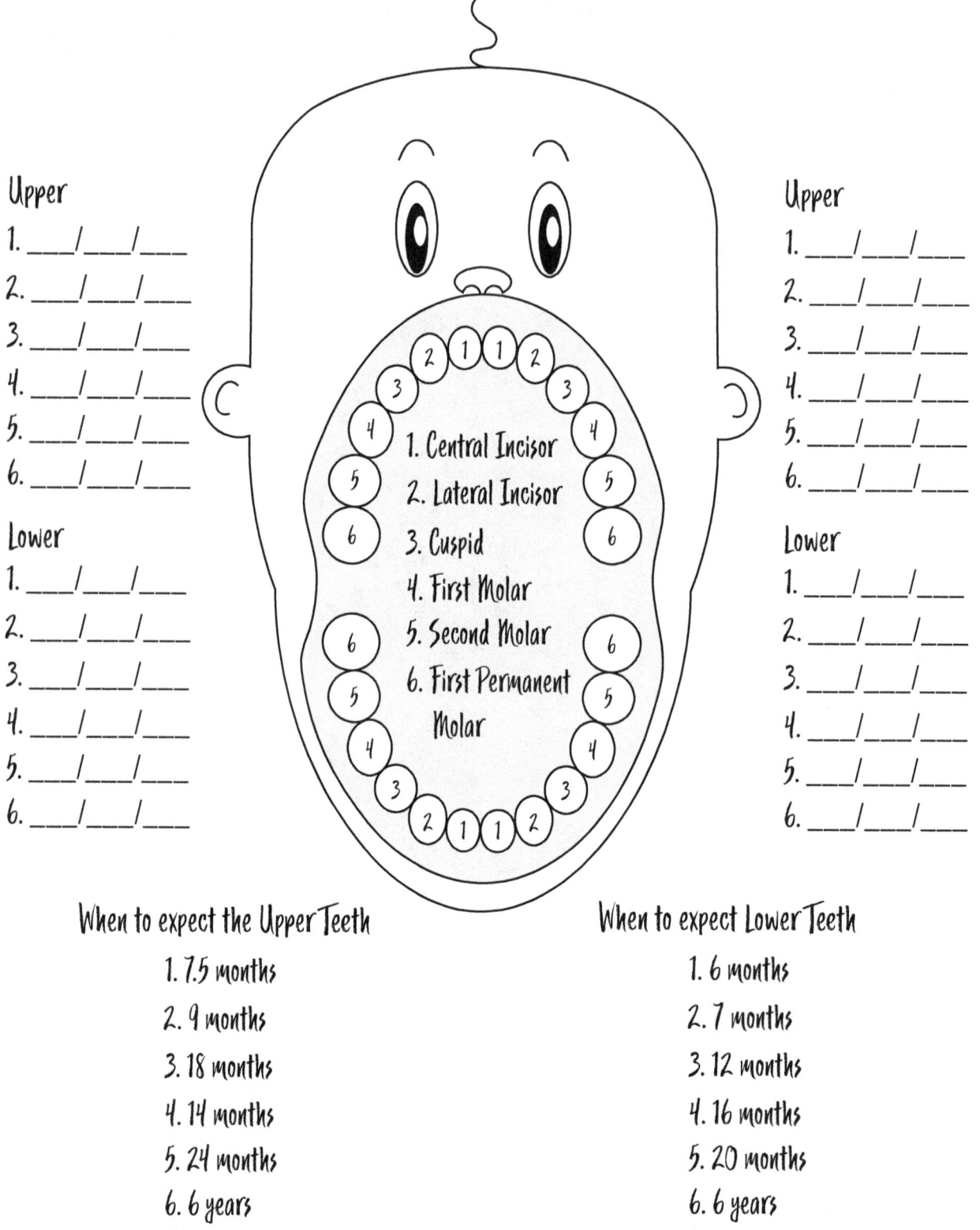

Medical Records

Date	Description

State Where You Live

State _____
Year of entrance into the Union _____
Capital _____
Population _____
Nickname _____
State Motto _____
State Bird _____
State Flower _____
State Mammal _____
Largest City _____
Famous people from this state _____
_____
_____

State Flag

States You Have Visited

	Date		Date
☐ Alabama	_____	☐ Montana	_____
☐ Alaska	_____	☐ Nebraska	_____
☐ Arizona	_____	☐ Nevada	_____
☐ Arkansas	_____	☐ New Hampshire	_____
☐ California	_____	☐ New Jersey	_____
☐ Colorado	_____	☐ New Mexico	_____
☐ Connecticut	_____	☐ New York	_____
☐ Deleware	_____	☐ North Carolina	_____
☐ Florida	_____	☐ North Dakota	_____
☐ Georgia	_____	☐ Ohio	_____
☐ Hawaii	_____	☐ Oklahoma	_____
☐ Idaho	_____	☐ Oregon	_____
☐ Illinois	_____	☐ Pennsylvania	_____
☐ Indiana	_____	☐ Rhode Island	_____
☐ Iowa	_____	☐ South Carolina	_____
☐ Kansas	_____	☐ South Dakota	_____
☐ Kentucky	_____	☐ Tennessee	_____
☐ Louisiana	_____	☐ Texas	_____
☐ Maine	_____	☐ Utah	_____
☐ Maryland	_____	☐ Vermont	_____
☐ Massachusetts	_____	☐ Virginia	_____
☐ Michigan	_____	☐ Washington	_____
☐ Minnesota	_____	☐ West Virginia	_____
☐ Mississippi	_____	☐ Wisconsin	_____
☐ Missouri	_____	☐ Wyoming	_____

Your First Year

1 Week	_____ pounds	_____ ounces
2 Weeks	_____ pounds	_____ ounces
3 Weeks	_____ pounds	_____ ounces
4 Weeks	_____ pounds	_____ ounces
1 Month	_____ pounds	_____ ounces
6 Weeks	_____ pounds	_____ ounces
2 Months	_____ pounds	_____ ounces
3 Months	_____ pounds	_____ ounces
4 Months	_____ pounds	_____ ounces
5 Months	_____ pounds	_____ ounces
6 Months	_____ pounds	_____ ounces
7 Months	_____ pounds	_____ ounces
8 Months	_____ pounds	_____ ounces
9 Months	_____ pounds	_____ ounces
10 Months	_____ pounds	_____ ounces
11 Months	_____ pounds	_____ ounces
12 Months	_____ pounds	_____ ounces

You Are Growing

Every Moment With You Is Cherished

Friends, Neighbors & Play Dates

Your Reaction to the Seasons

Family Vacations

Family Pics

Birthday Parties

One year old _____
_____
_____
_____

Two years old _____
_____
_____
_____

Three years old _____
_____
_____
_____

Four years old _____
_____
_____
_____

Five years old _____
_____
_____
_____

Party Pics

From Our Hearts to Yours

Our Journal Pages

Waiting is hard. Especially when you're waiting for something you've hoped and dreamed about for as long as you can remember. Our minds are filled with excitement and anticipation as we imagine what it will be like to see and hold you for the first time and bring you home. These next pages are journal entries sharing messages from our hearts...how we have felt and what it's been like going through the adoption process in our journey to you. We pray you know how much you have always been wanted and loved...and thank God for allowing us to be your forever mommy and daddy!

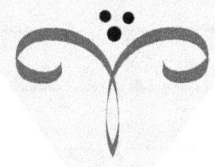

"Do not be anxious about anything, but in everything by prayer and supplication with thanksgiving let your requests be made known to God." ~Philippians 4:6 ESV

Date_____

_____
_____
_____
_____
_____
_____
_____
_____
_____
_____
_____

Date_____

_____
_____
_____
_____
_____
_____
_____
_____
_____
_____
_____

Date_____

_____
_____
_____
_____
_____
_____
_____
_____
_____
_____
_____

Date_____

_____
_____
_____
_____
_____
_____
_____
_____
_____
_____
_____

Date _____

_____
_____
_____
_____
_____
_____
_____
_____
_____

Date _____

_____
_____
_____
_____
_____
_____
_____
_____
_____

Date _____

_____
_____
_____
_____
_____
_____
_____
_____
_____

Date _____

_____
_____
_____
_____
_____
_____
_____
_____
_____

"May you always know my little one you were wished for, prayed for and wanted."
~Unknown

"Cast your cares on the Lord and He will sustain you, He will never let the righteous be shaken." ~Psalm 55:22

Date_____

Date_____

Date_____

Date_____

Date_____   Date_____

_____   _____
_____   _____
_____   _____
_____   _____
_____   _____
_____   _____
_____   _____
_____   _____
_____   _____
_____   _____

Date_____   Date_____

_____   _____
_____   _____
_____   _____
_____   _____
_____   _____
_____   _____
_____   _____
_____   _____
_____   _____
_____   _____

"Adoption is when a child grew in a mommy's heart instead of her tummy."
~Unknown

"May the God of hope fill you with all joy and peace as you trust in Him."
~Romans 15:13a

Date_____

_____
_____
_____
_____
_____
_____
_____
_____
_____
_____
_____
_____

Date_____

_____
_____
_____
_____
_____
_____
_____
_____
_____
_____
_____
_____

Date_____

_____
_____
_____
_____
_____
_____
_____
_____
_____
_____
_____
_____

Date_____

_____
_____
_____
_____
_____
_____
_____
_____
_____
_____
_____
_____

Date_____   Date_____

_____   _____
_____   _____
_____   _____
_____   _____
_____   _____
_____   _____
_____   _____
_____   _____
_____   _____
_____   _____

Date_____   Date_____

_____   _____
_____   _____
_____   _____
_____   _____
_____   _____
_____   _____
_____   _____
_____   _____
_____   _____
_____   _____

"God knit you together in your mother's womb, then He wove you into our hearts."
~Unknown

"I prayed for this child, and the Lord has granted me what I asked of Him."
~1 Samuel 1:27

Date_____

Date_____

Date_____

Date_____

Date _____

_____
_____
_____
_____
_____
_____
_____
_____
_____
_____

Date _____

_____
_____
_____
_____
_____
_____
_____
_____
_____
_____

Date _____

_____
_____
_____
_____
_____
_____
_____
_____
_____
_____

Date _____

_____
_____
_____
_____
_____
_____
_____
_____
_____
_____

"Every child deserves to be a dream come true."
~Unknown

"The Lord has done great things for us, and we are filled with joy."
~Psalm 126:3

Date_____

_____
_____
_____
_____
_____
_____
_____
_____
_____
_____
_____

Date_____

_____
_____
_____
_____
_____
_____
_____
_____
_____
_____
_____

Date_____

_____
_____
_____
_____
_____
_____
_____
_____
_____
_____
_____

Date_____

_____
_____
_____
_____
_____
_____
_____
_____
_____
_____
_____

Date_____   Date_____

Date_____   Date_____

"When you took your first breath, it took ours away."
~Unknown

"Start children off on the way they should go, and even when they are old they will not turn from it." ~Proverbs 22:6

Date_____

_____
_____
_____
_____
_____
_____
_____
_____
_____
_____

Date_____

_____
_____
_____
_____
_____
_____
_____
_____
_____
_____

Date_____

_____
_____
_____
_____
_____
_____
_____
_____
_____
_____

Date_____

_____
_____
_____
_____
_____
_____
_____
_____
_____
_____

Date_____

_____
_____
_____
_____
_____
_____
_____
_____
_____

Date_____

_____
_____
_____
_____
_____
_____
_____
_____
_____

Date_____

_____
_____
_____
_____
_____
_____
_____
_____
_____

Date_____

_____
_____
_____
_____
_____
_____
_____
_____
_____

"I'm in love with a child I haven't met yet."
~Unknown

"Rejoice in hope, be patient in tribulation, be constant in prayer."
~Romans 12:12 ESV

Date_____

_____
_____
_____
_____
_____
_____
_____
_____
_____
_____

Date_____

_____
_____
_____
_____
_____
_____
_____
_____
_____
_____

Date_____

_____
_____
_____
_____
_____
_____
_____
_____
_____
_____

Date_____

_____
_____
_____
_____
_____
_____
_____
_____
_____
_____

Date _____

_____
_____
_____
_____
_____
_____
_____
_____
_____
_____

Date _____

_____
_____
_____
_____
_____
_____
_____
_____
_____
_____

Date _____

_____
_____
_____
_____
_____
_____
_____
_____
_____
_____

Date _____

_____
_____
_____
_____
_____
_____
_____
_____
_____
_____

"Already in my heart...someday in my arms."
~Unknown

"Before I [God] formed you in the womb I knew you."
~Jeremiah 1:5a

Date_____

_____
_____
_____
_____
_____
_____
_____
_____
_____
_____

Date_____

_____
_____
_____
_____
_____
_____
_____
_____
_____
_____

Date_____

_____
_____
_____
_____
_____
_____
_____
_____
_____
_____

Date_____

_____
_____
_____
_____
_____
_____
_____
_____
_____
_____

Date _____

_____
_____
_____
_____
_____
_____
_____
_____
_____

Date _____

_____
_____
_____
_____
_____
_____
_____
_____
_____

Date _____

_____
_____
_____
_____
_____
_____
_____
_____
_____

Date _____

_____
_____
_____
_____
_____
_____
_____
_____
_____

"Every night I pray to God to keep you in His arms until I can hold you in mine."
~Unknown

"Every good gift and every perfect gift is from above."
~James 1:17a

Date_____ Date_____

_____ _____
_____ _____
_____ _____
_____ _____
_____ _____
_____ _____
_____ _____
_____ _____
_____ _____
_____ _____

Date_____ Date_____

_____ _____
_____ _____
_____ _____
_____ _____
_____ _____
_____ _____
_____ _____
_____ _____
_____ _____
_____ _____

Date_____

_____
_____
_____
_____
_____
_____
_____
_____
_____
_____

Date_____

_____
_____
_____
_____
_____
_____
_____
_____
_____
_____

Date_____

_____
_____
_____
_____
_____
_____
_____
_____
_____
_____

Date_____

_____
_____
_____
_____
_____
_____
_____
_____
_____
_____

"Every adoption story is beautiful, but ours is my favorite."
~Unknown

"Jesus told him, 'Don't be afraid; just believe'."
~Mark 5:36b

Date_____

_____
_____
_____
_____
_____
_____
_____
_____

Date_____

_____
_____
_____
_____
_____
_____
_____
_____

Date_____

_____
_____
_____
_____
_____
_____
_____
_____

Date_____

_____
_____
_____
_____
_____
_____
_____
_____

Date_____   Date_____

_____   _____
_____   _____
_____   _____
_____   _____
_____   _____
_____   _____
_____   _____
_____   _____
_____   _____
_____   _____

Date_____   Date_____

_____   _____
_____   _____
_____   _____
_____   _____
_____   _____
_____   _____
_____   _____
_____   _____
_____   _____
_____   _____

"God has perfect timing; never early, never late. It takes a little patience and a whole lot of faith…but it's worth the wait." ~Unknown

"But as for me and my household, we will serve the Lord."
~Joshua 24:15b

Date_____

_____
_____
_____
_____
_____
_____
_____
_____
_____
_____

Date_____

_____
_____
_____
_____
_____
_____
_____
_____
_____
_____

Date_____

_____
_____
_____
_____
_____
_____
_____
_____
_____
_____

Date_____

_____
_____
_____
_____
_____
_____
_____
_____
_____
_____

Date _____

_____
_____
_____
_____
_____
_____
_____
_____
_____

Date _____

_____
_____
_____
_____
_____
_____
_____
_____
_____

Date _____

_____
_____
_____
_____
_____
_____
_____
_____
_____

Date _____

_____
_____
_____
_____
_____
_____
_____
_____
_____

"You can't rush something you want to last forever."
~Unknown

"Whoever welcomes this child in My name welcomes Me [Jesus]."
~Luke 9:48a

Date_____

_____
_____
_____
_____
_____
_____
_____
_____
_____
_____

Date_____

_____
_____
_____
_____
_____
_____
_____
_____
_____
_____

Date_____

_____
_____
_____
_____
_____
_____
_____
_____
_____
_____

Date_____

_____
_____
_____
_____
_____
_____
_____
_____
_____
_____

Date _____   Date _____

Date _____   Date _____

"The adoption took time. The Love arrived instantly."
~Unknown

"...Be strong and courageous. Do not be afraid; do not be discouraged, for the Lord your God will be with you wherever you go." ~Joshua 1:9

Date_____

Date_____

Date_____

Date_____

Date _____

_____
_____
_____
_____
_____
_____
_____
_____
_____

Date _____

_____
_____
_____
_____
_____
_____
_____
_____
_____

Date _____

_____
_____
_____
_____
_____
_____
_____
_____
_____

Date _____

_____
_____
_____
_____
_____
_____
_____
_____
_____

"This is the start of our sweet little story...the part where your page meets ours."
~Unknown

"My flesh and my heart may fail, but God is the strength of my heart and my portion forever." ~Psalm 73:26

Date_____

_____
_____
_____
_____
_____
_____
_____
_____
_____
_____

Date_____

_____
_____
_____
_____
_____
_____
_____
_____
_____
_____

Date_____

_____
_____
_____
_____
_____
_____
_____
_____
_____
_____

Date_____

_____
_____
_____
_____
_____
_____
_____
_____
_____
_____

Date _____

_____
_____
_____
_____
_____
_____
_____
_____
_____
_____

Date _____

_____
_____
_____
_____
_____
_____
_____
_____
_____
_____

Date _____

_____
_____
_____
_____
_____
_____
_____
_____
_____
_____

Date _____

_____
_____
_____
_____
_____
_____
_____
_____
_____
_____

"Let love and faithfulness never leave you; bind them around your neck, write them on the tablet of your heart." ~Proverbs 3:3

"Children are a heritage from the Lord."
~Psalm 127:3a

Date_____

Date_____

Date_____

Date_____

Date _____

_____
_____
_____
_____
_____
_____
_____
_____
_____
_____
_____

Date _____

_____
_____
_____
_____
_____
_____
_____
_____
_____
_____
_____

Date _____

_____
_____
_____
_____
_____
_____
_____
_____
_____
_____
_____

Date _____

_____
_____
_____
_____
_____
_____
_____
_____
_____
_____
_____

"It's amazing how someone walks into your life and you can't remember how you ever lived without them." ~Unknown

"Take delight in the Lord and He will give you the desires of your heart."
~Psalm 37:4

Date_____

Date_____

Date_____

Date_____

Date_____

_____
_____
_____
_____
_____
_____
_____
_____
_____
_____
_____

Date_____

_____
_____
_____
_____
_____
_____
_____
_____
_____
_____
_____

Date_____

_____
_____
_____
_____
_____
_____
_____
_____
_____
_____
_____

Date_____

_____
_____
_____
_____
_____
_____
_____
_____
_____
_____
_____

"The Lord is good to those whose hope is in Him, to the one who seeks Him." ~Lamentations 3:25

"For I know the plans I have for you," declares the LORD, "plans to prosper you and not to harm you, plans to give you hope and a future." ~Jeremiah 29:11

Date_____

_____
_____
_____
_____
_____
_____
_____
_____
_____
_____
_____

Date_____

_____
_____
_____
_____
_____
_____
_____
_____
_____
_____
_____

Date_____

_____
_____
_____
_____
_____
_____
_____
_____
_____
_____
_____

Date_____

_____
_____
_____
_____
_____
_____
_____
_____
_____
_____
_____

Date_____   Date_____

Date_____   Date_____

"Bring joy to your servant, Lord, for I put my trust in You."
~Psalm 86:4

"May the God of hope fill you with all joy and peace as you trust in Him, so that you may overflow with hope by the power of the Holy Spirit." ~Romans 15:13

Date_____

_____
_____
_____
_____
_____
_____
_____
_____
_____
_____

Date_____

_____
_____
_____
_____
_____
_____
_____
_____
_____
_____

Date_____

_____
_____
_____
_____
_____
_____
_____
_____
_____
_____

Date_____

_____
_____
_____
_____
_____
_____
_____
_____
_____
_____

Date_____   Date_____

Date_____   Date_____

"Your [God's] eyes saw my unformed body; all the days ordained for me were written in Your book before one of them came to be." ~Psalm 139:16

www.ingramcontent.com/pod-product-compliance
Lightning Source LLC
Chambersburg PA
CBHW082105280426
43661CB00089B/870